ETHICAL MENTORSHIP

Missing Link in Transformational Leadership

CHARLES MWEWA

DEDICATION

For my "sons":

Humphrey Mutiti
Kasosa Mwinkeu
Misheck Nyendwa

CONTENTS

INTRODUCTION

Recent trends in terms of leadership are evolving around the concept of ethical mentorship in leadership. This phenomenon has permeated politics, corporations, humanitarian associations and, of course, regulatory formations.

In the past, focus was on the outcome to the total exclusion, at times, of the process. In a Machiavellian conception, people did not mind how the results were gotten, as long as the "end justified the means."

This, however, is no longer feasible, especially after the trendy movements of the Me-Too, the discovery of mass graves where Aboriginal children were indiscriminately buried in Canada, and the implication of the Catholic Fathers in the sexual abuses of children, etc.

There has been also an added layer of vigilance in the aftermath of the Trump presidency in the US which nearly abrogated all known ethical latitudes in the management of national affairs. And his popularity, notwithstanding, indicated that there had been a global and mental shift in the appreciation of ethics in the governance process.

Another event that had put a question mark on the reliance of transformational and visionary leadership to the negligence of moral and ethical predilections was the unilateral declaration of war by Russia and Putin in Ukraine. What began as a condemnation by strong and powerful nations had morphed into a norm and peoples and nations began to regard it as normal.

The last and probably the most important event which had global consequences is the twin upheaval of climate change and global warming. This has called for ethically-oriented leaders who understand that the activities of today have consequences on the populations of tomorrow. It is no longer what people do in one part of the globe; everything people do in one place affects everyone everywhere.

All these events, jointly and severally, call for a new type of leadership, ethical mentorship. This little book is an attempt at highlighting a new concept in transformational leadership – mentoring leadership – with an ethical predisposition. Inevitably, how this kind of leadership is accepted and implemented depends on various factors, including if this generation is willing to bequeath to the next ethical parameters that will sustain change and progress.

This book moves beyond the major mentoring models and theories which emphasize mentors (coaches)' goal-setting criteria towards the success of the mentees (clients)'s overall support through motivation, training, direction, and advising. The book assumes that the mentor has succeeded and that the client has been coached. The book goes a step further and focuses on the ethical leadership approach in the mentoring process and avouches that the major reason why theories and models on mentoring have not borne sustainable results is because of the absence of an ethical component on the part, mostly, of the coaches or mentors. The saliences briefly discussed in here are universal in nature and apply to all levels of leadership interactions.

cm.

1 | PROCESS-FOCUSED LEADERSHIP

Ethical Mentorship

There is a solution to the problem of corrupt leadership across the world. It is called Ethical Mentorship. Merriam-Webster Dictionary defines mentorship simply as "the influence, guidance, or direction given by a mentor." This is usually given by a mentor to someone who is less experienced or is *younger* than the mentor. Age is inconsequential; what matters is that what is given can sustain the future generations.

Panacea for Corruption

There are various levels of corruption in leadership – bribes, embezzlement of funds, financial mismanagement, fiscal miscalculations, misuse of donations, misappropriation of tithes and offerings, misdirection of funds to bogus spendings, maladjustments of taxes, and redirection of public or group money for private use, etc. Unethical leadership exists in every sector – politics, charities, businesses, academic, sports, recreation, entertainment, legal, clubs, churches, and mosques and synagogues, associations, private and public sectors. It is rampant in Africa, in Asia, in Europe, in the Americas, and across the islands and territories.

It is possible to be an effective leader without engaging in corrupt activities. All it takes is a strong adherence to ethical mentorship in the transaction of private and public affairs.

Process Not Necessarily the Result

Most of the incidents which involve corruption, and the unethical management of resources arise from the desire to avoid vilification and abuse. Such leaders usually want to project themselves as result-oriented. So, they may want to spend big, or to aim for wanton acquisitions. To such leaders, their personal image is more important than respect for process and procedure. They find it disabusing to project a wealthy front, even at the expense of other people's sweat, money, and sacrifices. Focusing on the process can ensure that good judgment and sobriety are preferred to showmanship and wanton disregard for ethics.

2 | OUTSOURCED ACCOUNTABILITY

Outsourced Accountability Processes

A leader cannot be an investigator, prosecutor, judge and jury and enforcer at the same time. Most corrupt bodies are organized on such premises. The leader is almost infallible and omnipotent; he or she does not seem to be accountable to anyone. And this lends itself to two scenarios.

Lack of Audit Processes

In the first scenario, the internal management mechanisms are created to give leadership no external audit subjection. The leader is usually deified as "General" something to create a vague ambience of general accountability. In this structure, the leader can do just about anything and is unaccountable to anybody.

This is akin to organizations and social associations in which leadership is enacted on a *laissez-faire* model. *Laissez-faire* leadership model, *per se*, is not inimical to good and accountable leadership. The tendency not to micromanage and the ability for the board not to get overtly involved in the day-to-day management of affairs are welcome approaches to leadership.

However, the *laissez faire* model in the absence of internal accountability mechanisms can be too damaging to an institution with unethical predispositions. Specificity must, therefore, be preferred in the assignment of leadership roles and functionality to curb this structural defect not to arbitrarily trusting a leader without strengthening accountability mechanisms. Even an angel can become a demon when given unlimited access to resources.

Broad Powers

In the second scenario, there are, in fact,

accountability mechanisms. However, the leader is assigned with broad and overarching powers that accountability is outrightly debased and rendered ineffective. This is akin to political leadership in which the leader is constitutionally given sets of unchallenged powers.

Absolute power usually damages morals. It is in the best interest of both the leader and the organization that powers be evenly distributed across many vents so that each dimension or level of leadership is accountable to real people or substructural formations or boards of auditors. Those who define and assign powers must be wary of this potential human weakness. Power should not be dispensed liberally; there should be fundamental limits and ethical protections.

3 | THE MAGIC OF COMPLIANCE

Compliance Not Only Obedience

Compliance and obedience are not the same. The two are not the same as quality control measurement mechanisms in leadership parlance. Obedience applies more to God or to filial arrangements than to organizational or corporate entities. Thus, we ought to obey God unequivocally but men only reasonably.

Dangers of Obedience

We should not obey fellow human beings unequivocally – because, like us, they are fallible. The impression created in corporate and organizational leadership is that the leader is like a god, clustered in such hefty but parochial titles like "boss," "leader," "patron," "father," "general overseer," etc.

The connotation here is that nothing happens or can move on or succeed without either the blessing or presence of *this* leader. This type of leadership formation requires absolute dedication to the leader and not to the process. In many cases, when such a leader dies or is incapacitated, the entire corporation or organization falls apart or crumbles.

And it has a weakness; due to its obedience modeling, the leadership in place rarely creates a succession mechanism, leaving the system to morph through, traditionally, as a family arrangement or affair. Thus, in case of the demise of the "leader," an impromptu and sometimes a make-shift succession process occurs in which the more likely to succeed is the person who happens to witness the demise of the leader, usually, his or her spouse or children than men and women of elevated moral and ethical principles. And since such inheritors did not share the raw vision for the organization, the dream dies with the "leader."

This has been the case in many nongovernmental organizations, church orders and African political establishments (there are some exceptions), where successors have not been able to emulate or replicate the same success as the founder or dominant "leader" had before them. Sycophants rarely make good leaders – because by their very nature, they are a scheme based on "leader" worship and submission.

Durability of Compliance

Compliance, on the other hand, is a more reliable method as a quality control measurement mechanism in leadership parlance than obedience. It fosters strict adherence to a procedural constituted policy, usually enacted by consensus.

To comply entails following a clear procedure and is, usually, done in the best interest of the corporation or organization, and not only the individual leader. Therefore, compliance requires that there are a set of rules or principles which apply to all, irrespective of position or seniority. They are, as it were, a democratic means of governing a public interest or corporate entity.

For a church, that might mean establishing a set of ecclesiastical guidelines applicable to all – to the leader and followers alike. For a national government – the constitution must be enacted in such a way that it gives no leverage to one individual at the expense of the entire nation.

For Africa, this is an urgent need. Africa, in general, inherited, or instituted colonial-based constitutions which gave unnecessary powers to one individual or the president or prime minister. The colonial idea was to create post-colonial African states that would continue to be dominated, economically, by their former masters. The best way to do so was to insist on constitutions which concentrated power in an individual the former colonial masters could directly control and not in a system they could not directly control.

Thus, in most African constitutions, a president can do almost anything without any accountability. Some countries have lifted immunities after the fact, but that is only after damage has already been done. And the hypocrisy of the West is that they, themselves have constitutions that give very little powers to their president or prime minister.

And this has had the effect of increased accountability and lessened incidents of corruption in the public sector in western formations. Similarly, church leaders in the

West are less prone to corruption than their African counterparts because they are subjected to compliance mechanisms.

No matter how shielded from corruption in the West they may be, compliance does not seem to weed out discrimination and prejudice. Compliance mechanisms in western formations dither at the implementation level – because the same rule may be applied differently to different people depending on race, color, national original, disability or ability, etc. This danger exists in all former colonial master countries, and it requires deliberate legislation and attitudinal reformation to be restrained.

4 | POSITIONAL INFLUENCE

Deweaponization of Positional Influence

Influence is relative. Every position comes with its own sphere and influence. The general rule is that each position is a privilege and an opportunity to do right. Even corrupt leaders understand this fact. But then they ignore it. They use the influence that the position brings to circumvent punishments and rewards to their advantage. Corrupt leaders weaponize their positions in the following three ways: weaponized authority, demand for total obedience; and sanitized indecency.

Weaponized Authority

First, they weaponize authority. This is the key entrance to their means of voice sabotage and mind control. Those they lead are not given a choice to think rationally and independently. They claim that they have arrogated authority and that they can use it anyhow they wish. Followers do believe and comply, thereby giving corrupt leaders an unfettered discretion on how they use corporate or group resources.

Demand for Total Obedience

Second, they demand total obedience. In one way or the other, said or unsaid, explicit or implied, corrupt leaders demand that they are obeyed without question. They may justify obedience based on some usurped, bequeathed, or divine authority.

In such organizations as organized criminality, religion or even in politics, leaders may variously demand that their followers or clients obey them without question and claim that God, or guns or the "people" have given them such authority.

Sanitized Indecency

And third, they sanitize indecency. They cultivate a culture of lewdness in which decency is managed and truth is economized. This is done to prevent their followers from asking tough questions. In many situations, the followers, or clients are involved and do share in the *proceeds of crime* or the corrupt rewards. Thus, followers or clients may be silenced permanently.

Proposed Solutions

The solution to the weaponization of positional influence lies in the normalization of positional authority through checks and balances. Humans are prone to corruption if left unchallenged. The following three are how a leader can be equipped to display ethical leadership using their positional influence: normalization, formalization, and deweaponization.

Normalization

First, by normalizing positional authority. Every position must be subjected to public scrutiny or tender or sectorial review. Many organizations, and even governments, have circumvented this by giving the leader broad vetting powers. In other words, the leader is the process itself.

Such leaders can determine how to evaluate a scheme and even how to award incentives. For example, in many national constitutions, the president is the one who appoints, vets, and ratifies the vetters. Similarly, in many organizations, vetters may be appointed by the chairperson, to whom they also report. In both scenarios, checks are offset by balances. And as a result, such setups breed unethical systems.

Formalization

Second, there ought to be some formal leadership grooming or appointing process, such as interviews or regulations. A criterion for progressive disciplinary regime which includes everyone in the organization or nation must be designed. In politics, the concept of the Rule of Law is sufficient for such processes.

In religious organizations, submission to an authoritative book, such as the Bible or Quran may be sufficient only if it is supplemented by the oversight of an authoritative, independent, or autonomous body. In other organizations, a constitution or sets of by-laws or a moral or ethical code of conduct should be used to manage organizational behavior and order.

Deweaponization

And third, positional influence should not be weaponized against the very interest it purports to serve. Ethical mentoring in leadership entails an adherence to a set of written or unwritten moral rules based on the idea of right and *not* good. The idea of right is a principled-based strategy that is aimed at meeting the needs of the organization without sacrificing goodness.

The idea of *good* is usually a personalized approach to leadership that, in many ways, sacrifices right. Hence, when a leader is called upon to decide, they should first do *right* before *good*. Goodness is desired; rightness is presumed. And right is what a committee, board, assembly, or the people say it is.

For organized religion or associations and public bodies, the authority that defines rightness must be unequivocal and a direct product of group or divine consensus. The idea of right cannot be left to the definitive will of a single leader, no matter how virtuous.

5 | CONCEPT OF RIGHT

Exemplification of the Right Concept

There have been recent writings about risk-taking as an active leadership trait. However, that is only in so far as the pursuit of right is the motivating factor behind risk-taking. Right is might. And it is preferable to risk-taking.

True ethical leadership exemplifies right in file and rank. Right is the mantra, the *sine qua non* of governance. It is essential, and necessary for any definition of leadership to be moral. Right is the key ingredient in any leadership formulation; without it, any leadership structure crumbles. There is no justification for not doing *right*.

Right may be a philosophical construct, but its application is widely acknowledged as mundane and even common. In all forms of organized societies and civilizations, right is the first concept that is enshrined in the consciousness of children. They understand, from the beginning, that there is a difference between right and wrong. This understanding even precedes the differentiation between good and bad. It is, in fact, because people first learn the differences between right and wrong that they can later conceive the differences between good and evil. Right presupposes good.

Facets of Right

There are fundamentally six facets of right. First, the least level of leadership is when a leader breaks the rules of right behavior and teaches others to do the same. A leader is a model of right behavior. Whether that is in corporate, national, or family and organizational setting, leadership should rise above the petty, lead above the fray and demonstrate right in all its dealings.

There would be no need to follow if leadership was understood to showcase wrong. People can surrender their very rights so long as they understand that leadership means well for them. There is always a presumption that leadership will do right – because it must.

Leadership must be premised on right. It follows, therefore, that when a leader is corrupt or harbors unethical tendencies, he or she does not only break the rule of right, but in so doing, they also demonstrate that others could break the rules or ethical order.

Actions are as words, behavior as attitude, in leadership.

One does not delineate from one without the other. Everything the leader does or says is being emulated by someone in the organization or the public, for good or for worse.

Second, leadership is an obligation to instruct others into the right behavior and right living. The threshold, thus, created, is higher than the position held. Leadership is an effective instruction process. In short, leaders are teachers. They teach both with words and actions.

Leadership that is unethical can eventually breed corruption, poverty, and disillusionment. It is not the good of a leader but the right of the followers that matters. Followers are the purpose for which leadership exists. When their good is frustrated, the right of a leader to lead is muted.

Third, right must be practiced so that it benefits all. It cannot only be right for others and not for the leader. Many times, leaders, indeed, preach and even publicly showcase right. But they may not practice right themselves, especially when no-one is observing. There is no economy in the practice of right; it must be done as they say, "in season and out of season." Every leader must understand that they must always do right – whether they are being monitored or not.

The people the leader has charge over are entrusted to the leader in good faith. They are not to be abused or taken advantage of, however vulnerable or powerless they might be. The leader must not take away their rights, liberties, freedoms, joys, moneys, or resources at will.

The leader must not use people as his or her own assets, either. Doing right means preserving the integrity, wholeness, dreams, dignity, and property of the followers. And leaders must shun away from creating innuendos and stratagems of how they could defraud the people they lead, such as creating fake problems they want to solve, or justifying their wanton for gain using God or "the people" excuses. Ethical leadership respects the freedom of followers.

Fourth, leadership must be the pursuit of what is right. It is understandable that the leader, being human, may fumble and falter, from time to time, as they try to lead by example. However, they must rise, re-order themselves and continue the path of right.

Leadership is the ability, by the leader, to do all and everything, to maintain right. Mistakes may be made, but it should be the duty and desire of the leader to rectify those mistakes and reinstitute right. For example, when a leader does or says something that is wrong, it is the responsibility of the leader to apologize and seek to return into the right lane. A leader must not stop pursuing the ideals of right.

Fifth, *righteous* acts exemplify an attitude of integrity and wholeness. Integrity and wholeness are abstract concepts unless they are exemplified through right. Someone cannot say that they have integrity if their actions and attitudes showcase wrong. Leadership's claim to integrity must be viewed through the lens of right living, right behavior, and right attitudes. Leadership is mastery over right and abhorrence over vice. There is no middle ground, if one does not do or practice right, one is doing or practicing wrong.

And sixth, right is impartial, because right and justice are co-foundations of a moral society. A corrupt leader is, in fact, a selfish leader – because they allow their personal enjoyment to override the general good.

All leadership levels are equal. Any leadership obligation (at cell, team, organizational, regional, national, or international levels) is an opportunity to do just and right. Leaders do not take sides unless that side is one of right.

In other words, leaders must always lean towards right. Right does not discriminate, does not take biased positions, and does not unfairly treat others. Right is fair and impartial, all the time.

6 | THE PURSUIT OF WHOLENESS

What Ethical Mentorship is Not

Ethical leadership is not one of the following four indices: It is not the realization of perfection; it is not the actualization of total honesty; it is not the exemplification of perpetual faultlessness; and it is not a characterization of unmatched integrity. Ethical leadership is all these blended in moderate synchronicity.

Pursuit of Perfection

A leader who desires to model wholeness must not be judged on the scale of what is but of what ought to be. Pursuit is the defining characteristic of whole leadership.

Ethical leaders pursue perfection. They are not perfect. They make it a goal to go for it. They cannot be held to a standard of having reached it. They should not be indicted on the bench of exactness.

No leader, whether just beginning or is an experienced veteran, is equipped to reach such standards. However, any leader worth his or her salt should strive daily to reach that standard. Because they are not expected to have reached such a standard, ethical leaders should know their limitations and acknowledge that they cannot do it all. This realization is key to being able to define their own involvement in goal setting, implementation and the results expected.

There is always room to grow, to learn in the process, and even to fail. Failing in achieving a goal does not mean that a leader is a failure; failure may be the very incentive that promotes creativity and leads to goal accomplishment. The important question is not: Will a leader fail? But the question is: What does a leader learn from failure?

Pursuit of Honesty

While truth may not be economized, honesty can be managed. It is the management of honesty that sets one leader above the other. Honesty is multilayered. It exists at personal (internal), relational, corporate (communal), and psychic (mental, intellectual, or spiritual) levels. It is the agreement reached by an individual that they will be open about their dealings – privately and publicly.

Honesty and truth are related, but they are not the same. Truth is absolute and does not change to fit any *agenda*. Honesty can be managed to portray truth in any different light. Thus, a person may honestly tell a lie, but truth does not lie.

The imperative of honesty is its purpose. When truth has been established, honesty is that act or word or sequence of events that agrees with that truth. A person is, therefore, being honest if they declare the truth of a matter, in any given circumstance. For example, if money has been embezzled and there is established or presumed evidence that a leader did it, an honest leader will take responsibility for it.

Honesty means that the leader agrees with

the established reality and admits to the truth. Similarly, a leader could be lying and be totally honest about it; and could be telling the truth and be dishonest about it. The relativity of honesty and the absoluteness of truth render these dichotomous relatives an essence of leadership.

Ethical leadership pursues honesty in the spirit of truth. In other words, *an ethical leader may circumvent honesty to maintain truth*. He or she is honest because they want to maintain the truth. If honesty hurts truth, it is not desired honesty. However, truth may hurt honesty for the purpose of sustaining or protecting the truth. Accordingly, *a leader who is dishonest to protect truth, is an ethical leader.*

A leader who is honest to hurt truth, may be unethical. For example, the courts may honestly refuse to disclose the identity of a minor child to protect the truth. And the truth could be that, if disclosed, the minor might be harmed. So, the courts are not being honest but truthful. Ethical leaders should do the same; they should protect the truth with relative honesty.

Pursuit of Faultlessness

Ethical leadership is not the absence of

fault. It is being in pursuit of faultlessness. A leader will, from time to time, default in their moral pursuit. They may be mistaken, blameworthy and even immoral, from time to time. But this should be a natural consequence of their pursuit of faultlessness. The fault should be attributable to action and not to lack of it, to a desire to actualize and not the absence of it.

Leadership is by character dynamic. If it is not, nothing tangible can be accomplished. Leaders should make many attempts, take many risks, try many combinations, and pursue many avenues. They cannot simply wait for the opportune time or moment. When one such moment comes, they, of course, should not dawdle. Leadership must always be on the move.

In the journey called leadership, there are many detours and impediments. There are obstacles and unexpected moments. Leadership is not linear. There is no single formula that balances up to leadership. There are signposts, and that is what there are. These signposts provide guidelines and principles that ensure that the destination is sure. However, even in the application of such leadership points as vision, tenacity, intelligence, rightness, or justice, the permutations are not universally deterministic.

The leader must always try something. When mistakes are made, they must be made in the quest to reach the end of leadership, which is the accomplishment of pre-identified goals. The ideal for the leader is to reach the end of leadership without any hiccups or making a single mistake. However, experientially, and practically, that is not attainable. A determined leader should not be deterred by this fact but should stand on this fact to reach the end of leadership without detouring, fumbling, or defaulting. This defines the pursuit of faultlessness.

Pursuit of Integrity

Humanity survives on relative wholeness, and not on absolute wholeness. One may be whole in spirit but bleeding in body and mind. They may be whole in their mind but aching in their soul and body, etc. This is similar when it comes to the fundamentals of moral and behavioral wellness. While relative wellness is possible, absolute wellness is a pipedream. Relative wholeness or wellness can lead to soundness, which is a state of being whole in relative terms to key functionalities in the human body or in life.

When someone asks: "How are you?" and another responds: "I am well, thank you." "I am well," is in reference to one's general wellness or wholeness and not to the particulars of one's wellness relative to their bodies, minds, finances, family, intellect, etc. If probed further, one may discover that although they responded that they were well, something deep within or in their relationship or in their finances or in their health, etc., might be incomplete and in need of checking.

In terms of character and good behavior, the same concept of wholeness applies. No-one can say that they are whole one hundred percent of the time in their character and behavior. They may only be so relative to their mood, personality, interpersonal interactions, societal attitude, upbring and background and, whether they are alone or in public. Some people are very good at modelling the best of themselves in character terms in public but harbor dangerous and distasteful habits and tendencies when they are alone or in private.

Ethical leaders pursue wholeness or the attainment of unmatched integrity as a daily goal. While wholeness is a state, integrity is a value or a quality of something. Most dictionaries equate value or quality to being honest or to having some strong moral principles. As reviewed earlier, honesty is never absolute; it can only be relatable. The dictionary definition of integrity comes up short on the real understanding of integrity. For a leader with integrity, being honest is not enough; being whole is assumed.

Both words, that is, *integrity* and *wholeness*, do not involve a multiplicity of parts augmenting and coming together. Only integrity may reach that threshold. Wholeness defines *a state of one part involving many*. But integrity defines *different parts coming together as one*.

The root word, "integral" applies to integrity. And, in essence, it denotes necessity. Integrity deals with the aspects of behavior that are essential or necessary to morality and character. They are part of a good and acceptable moral conduct. A person or leader with integrity integrates good conduct, has a sound moral campus, and can add value to the way he or she relates to people.

There is no production of an individual of integrity without first the internalization of sound and good moral behavior. A leader who has not internalized respectable behaviors is incapable of bringing forth an integrated personality.

An immoral leader may attempt to be and

look good for a while, but they will immediately succumb to the internalized immoral predilections.

Similarly, a leader who has been schooled in the intricacies of sound and moral behavior may falter, and fail, from time to time, but they will eventually return to sane and moral behavior.

In essence, when a leader is corrupt and continues to be corrupt, it means that *internally*, they are incapable of being anything else. This does not mean that reform or redemption is not possible. But unless such rehabilitation or redemption is genuine, they will continue to revert to corrupt, immoral practices.

On the other hand, if a child has been brought up "integrating" different parts of good and moral behavior, internally, they may continue to desire to do and remain on the moral trajectory even when they may succumb to immorality, from time to time. And the reason is because their internal mechanism is predisposed to desiring moral uprightness, and to be consistent and uncompromising in their adherence to strong moral and ethical principles and values.

A leader who is whole and has integrity may not behave the same with other people's money, property, sexuality, or assets. That is because they may realize that they have a relationship of trust – which is a hallmark of an integrated whole.

An unintegrated whole may create an internal conscience which is at odds with the type of behavior that is contrary to sound moral principles. It may also go against societal norms.

Moral and ethical leadership is, therefore, not groomed when in a leadership capacity but outside of it. Good and moral leaders are made before they lead. The duty of the electorate, for example, is to recognize such and elect or vote for them or appoint them in office. They might have defaulted or done something wrong before because it is inevitable. However, they would have already internalized and integrated good traits that would make them ethical leaders.

Truth about Rehabilitation

There are three irrefutable truths regarding repentance, rehabilitation, reformation, or change. First, good people may do bad things. Second, bad people may do good things. And three, people change.

It is important that society or an

organization does not neglect to factor in these three truths in making character decisions. Some people may not currently be as they acted in the past. Some may have acted better in the past, but they currently harbor bad behaviors. And others may not show any signs of bad or good character.

Ex-convicts, for example, should not be impeached because of their criminal records. Those with past disciplinary records or with one or two indecent behavioral instances should not be ostracized, either. Such people might have reformed for the better.

A line is, therefore, drawn between what is and what ought to be. What is may not always be what is ought to be. And what is ought to be may not always be what is. It calls for sound good judgment to fairly determine human character.

ABOUT THE AUTHOR

Charles Mwewa (LLB; BA Law; BA Ed; LLM) is a prolific author and researcher, poet, novelist, lawyer, law professor and Christian apologist. Mwewa has written no less than 40 books and counting in every genre and has exhibited his works at prestigious expos like the Ottawa International Book Expo and is the winner of the Coppa Awards for his signature publication, *Zambia: Struggles of My People.*

SELECTED BOOKS BY THIS AUTHOR

1. *ZAMBIA: Struggles of My People (First and Second Editions)*
2. *10 FINANCIAL & WEALTH ATTITUDES TO AVOID*
3. *10 STRATEGIES TO DEFEAT STRESS AND DEPRESSION: Creating an Internal Safeguard against Stress and Depression*
4. *100+ REASONS TO READ BOOKS*
5. *A CASE FOR AFRICA?S LIBERTY: The Synergistic Transformation of Africa and the West into First-World Partnerships*
6. *A PANDEMIC POETRY, COVID-19*
7. *ALLERGIC TO CORRUPTION: The Legacy of President Michael Sata of Zambia*
8. *BOOK ABOUT SOMETHING: On Ultimate Purpose*
9. *CAMPAIGN FOR AFRICA: A Provocative Crusade for the Economic and Humanitarian Decolonization of Africa*
10. *CHAMPIONS: Application of Common Sense and Biblical Motifs to Succeed in Both Worlds*
11. *CORONAVIRUS PRAYERS*
12. *HH IS THE RIGHT MAN FOR ZAMBIA: And Other Acclaimed Articles on Zambia and Africa*
13. *I BOW: 3500 Prayer Lines of Inspiration & Intercession from the Heart: Volume One*
14. *INTERUNIVERSALISM IN A NUTSHELL: For Iranian Refugee Claimants*
15. *LAW & GRACE: An Expository Study in the Rudiments of Sin and Truth*
16. *LAWS OF INFLUENCE: 7even Lessons in Transformational Leadership*

17. *LOVE IDEAS IN COVID PANDEMIC TIMES: For Couples & Lovers*
18. *P.A.S.S: Version 2: Answer Bank*
19. *P.A.S.S.: Acing the Ontario Paralegal-Licensing Examination, Version 2*
20. *POETRY: The Best of Charles Mwewa*
21. *QUOT-EBOS: Essential. Barbs. Opinions. Sayings*
22. *REASONING WITH GOD IN PRAYER: Poetic Verses for Peace & Unconfronted Controversies*
23. *RESURRECTION: (A Spy in Hell Novel)*
24. *I DREAM OF AFRICA: Poetry of Post-Independence Africa, the Case of Zambia*
25. *SERMONS: Application of Legal Principles and Procedures in the Life and Ministry of Christ*
26. *SONG OF AN ALIEN: Over 130 Poems of Love, Romance, Passion, Politics, and Life in its Complexity*
27. *TEMPORARY RESIDENCE APPLICATION*
28. *THE GRACE DEVOTIONAL: Fifty-two Happy Weeks with God*
29. *THE SYSTEM: How Society Defines & Confines Us: A Worksheet*
30. *FAIRER THAN GRACE: My Deepest for His Highest*
31. *WEALTH THINKING: And the Concept of Capisolism*
32. *PRAYER: All Prayer Makes All Things Possible*
33. *PRAYER: All Prayer Makes All Things Possible, Answers*
34. *PRISONER OF GRACE: An I Saw Jesus at Milton Vision*
35. *PRAYERS OF OUR CHILDREN*
36. *VALLEY OF ROSES: City Called Beautiful*
37. *THE PATCH THEOREM: A Philosophy of Death, Life and Time*
38. *50 RULES OF POLITICS: A Rule Guide on Politics*
39. *ALLERGIC TO CORRUPTION: The Legacy of*

INDEX

donations, 2

guns, 16

E

ecclesiastical guidelines, 11
embezzlement, 2
enforcer. *See* accountable
ethical mentorship, vii
ethical order, 23
ethical principles, 10, 35
Europe, 2

F

failure, 28
fair. *See* discriminate
family, 10, 22, 33
father. *See* titles
faultlessness, 27, 31, 32
finances, 33
fiscal miscalculations, 2
followers, 12, 16, 17, 23, 24
formalization, 17
formula, 31
freedoms. *See* liberties

G

general overseer. *See* titles
global warming. *See* ethical
    mentorship
goals, 32
good faith, 24
good judgment, 3, 37

H

health, 33
honesty, 27, 29, 30, 34
humanitarian associations.
    See ethical mentorship
hypocrisy, 12

I

immorality, 35
impartial. *See* discriminate
impediments, 31
implementation, 13, 28
indecency, 15, 17
infallible. *See* accountable
influence, 15
integrity, 24, 25, 27, 33, 34, 35
investigator. *See* accountable
islands, 2

J

joys, 24
judge. *See* accountable
jury. *See* accountable
justice, 26, 31

L

laissez-faire model, 6
law, 39

www.ingramcontent.com/pod-product-compliance
Lightning Source LLC
Chambersburg PA
CBHW071516030726
47593CB00003B/1286